Original title:
Gingerbread Wishes and Holiday Kisses

Author: Dante Kingsley
ISBN HARDBACK: 978-9916-90-858-7
ISBN PAPERBACK: 978-9916-90-859-4

The Elegant Thread of Sugar and Spice

In a kitchen where chaos reigns,
Flour flies like snow, oh the pains.
Sprinkles dance in a merry swirl,
As I trip over my cat's playful twirl.

The dough's too sticky, my hands are glue,
Trying to shape a snowman that's new.
But it looks like a blob, all flat and wide,
Is it a treat or a giant slide?

The frosting's fighting, like cats in a tree,
One side's pink, the other green spree.
I meant to write 'Cheer' but it says 'Weird',
My cookie's a horror, but I persevered!

With laughter ringing through the bright night,
My friends all giggle at my silly sight.
We toast with hot cocoa, hearts so light,
In this bake-off chaos, everything's alright!

Scented Secrets by the Glow of the Fire

In the kitchen, things get wild,
Sugar flops and laughter piled.
Fuzzy socks and flour fight,
Marshmallows take a daring flight.

Whisking dreams with giggles sweet,
Spiced aromas, oh what a treat!
Cookies leap from trays with glee,
Who knew baking could be so free?

Delightful Moments Wrapped in Warmth

Hot cocoa spills, a chocolate flood,
Sipping slow, but there's a thud.
A marshmallow plops in my tea,
Now it's swimming, oh, woe is me!

Blankets tangled, a snuggly fight,
Tickles and laughs last through the night.
Hiding treats behind our backs,
Whoops! I think we've lost the snacks!

Sugar-kissed Smiles in the Chill

Snowflakes dance, a giggling cheer,
Frosty noses, hot drinks near.
Sleds go zooming down the hill,
Each bump, each shout, oh what a thrill!

Candy canes and silly hats,
Felines chasing fluffy rats.
Add sprinkles to the frosty air,
Laughter sparkles everywhere!

Enchantment of Winter's Crunchy Bites

Crispy treats that giggle loud,
Piled high, they draw a crowd.
Who can resist a crunchy prize?
With every nibble, laughter flies!

Cookies form a jolly troupe,
Dancing 'round the melted scoop.
With sugar ants and sticky hands,
The funniest mess in cookie lands!

Mirthful Sweets on a Frosty Eve

Frosty windows, laughter high,
Cookies dancing, oh my, oh my!
Spices sprinkle, cheerful cheer,
As we munch, the joy draws near.

Sneaky elves in hats so bright,
Dip their toes in the festive night.
Marshmallows plump, smiles on a spree,
Who needs snow? Just give me glee!

Joy in Every Flake and Sparkle

Snowflakes twirl, like gumdrops fly,
In this chaos, we can't deny.
A candy cane with a twisty grin,
Join the fun, let the giggles begin!

Frosted cakes adorned with flair,
Laughter echoes through the air.
With silly hats and mittens wide,
We'll ride this sugar-coated slide!

Love's Flavors in a Cozy Embrace

Warm hugs wrapped in tart surprise,
Chuckle here while chili fries.
Cinnamon dreams and nutty schemes,
Feeding hearts with tasty beams.

Giggles burst from every mug,
Sloppy kisses, snug as a bug.
Fudge and fun become the norm,
In sugary joy, we all transform!

Together in Tinsel and Treats

Tinsel glimmers, cookies call,
Sweet little bites, come one and all!
Sprinkle laughter with every bite,
Chocolate stains are pure delight.

With each crunch, our spirits soar,
Caramel laughter ev'ry door.
Let's toast to fun in sticky glee,
Sharing sweets, just you and me!

Warmth of the Oven in the Cool of Night

In a kitchen bright and merry,
The flour flies and things get hairy.
Cookies dance, oh what a sight,
Sugar sprinkles, pure delight.

Mom's wearing a hat that's far too big,
While Dad's on a mission, doing a jig.
The timer dings, the treats now rise,
We hold our breath, oh what a prize!

Nuance of Nutmeg in Every Laughter

Nutmeg sprinkles and laughter loud,
Grandma's stories always draw a crowd.
With each chuckle, scents arise,
The spices waft as joy complies.

The dog steals a treat, oh what a thief!
While Auntie giggles, shaking in disbelief.
Around the table, the fun won't crack,
Everyone's laughing; there's no looking back.

Craving Comfort in a Cup

Hot cocoa swirls in a fluffy mug,
Topped with mini marshmallows, a squishy hug.
With every sip, the warmth pours in,
In this cozy corner, we all break grins.

A cocoa mustache? Oh what a look!
As we gather 'round with a favorite book.
Each silly face deserves a freeze,
During these moments, we sip with ease.

Delicious Echoes of the Past

Back in time, we made a mess,
Sprinkling sugar, oh what success!
The kitchen filled with giggles and crumbs,
As memories baked, sweet smiles hum.

The cat stole a cookie, with sneaky flair,
Leaving us laughing, our worries laid bare.
With every recipe, a tale retold,
In the warmth of love, memories unfold.

Candied Moments and Shimmering Stars

In a kitchen, chaos reigns,
Flour flies and sugar gains,
Baking mishaps, what a sight,
A cookie fight, oh what delight!

Rolling dough with glee and cheer,
Sprinkled laughter fills the sphere,
Peeking in, the oven's hot,
A ginger ensemble, quite the plot!

Sticky hands, a chocolate war,
Icing battles, who could ask for more?
One too many sprinkles here,
A tasty mess, it seems quite clear!

So here's to sweets and giggles shared,
Tasty dreams, and none are spared,
With laughter loud and hearts aglow,
This recipe of joy we know!

The Hearth's Glow and Sweet Composure

Gather round, the hearth does gleam,
Baking goods, a fluttering dream,
Cookies line the counter bold,
A tale of sugar, spice, and gold!

Whisking dreams with candy flair,
Flavors dancing in the air,
An epic clash of chocolate chips,
And doughnuts made with donut strips!

Bartering sweets like little kids,
Trading cookies, oh what bids!
Giggles burst as we all taste,
In this kitchen, no one's waste!

Jolly cheers as friends partake,
Every bite, a laugh to make,
In this warm, delightful space,
Sweet concoctions with silly grace!

Sweetheart Confections and Illuminated Hearts

Cakes that wobble, oh so sweet,
An army formed of gummy treat,
Lollipops, they wield their charm,
A sugar fight that brings no harm!

Cupcake capers, sprinkles fly,
Marshmallow clouds drift in the sky,
Flavor pokes and yellow goo,
A frosted mess, but we all knew!

Chocolate rivers, okay, more like trays,
Maple syrup, oh what a craze,
Each confection, a gag and grin,
With every bite, we laugh and spin!

Watch the frosting swirl and dive,
This holiday spirit makes us thrive,
With brightened smiles and sugar spins,
In these moments, joy begins!

Happy Sprinkles and Friendly Faces

Sprinkles rain like colorful confetti,
Baking blunders get us all jetty,
A frosted fiasco, oh what fun,
Sweet surprises, oh aren't we done?

Piping bags with laughter stuffed,
Every mishap, oh, aren't we tough?
Icing fingers as we all create,
Silly snacks on every plate!

A ginger disaster turns to gold,
Each shared bite warms hearts tenfold,
The more we taste, the more we cheer,
In this kitchen, joy is near!

So toast to sweets and crazy plays,
With every batch, our worries blaze,
With friendly faces, our laughter rolls,
As happy sprinkles hug our souls!

Charmed by Sprinkles and Soft Frost

In the kitchen, a dance with dough,
Rolling out fun, watch the flour blow!
Cinnamon giggles, as sugar likes to play,
How many laughs in this dough-filled ballet?

With icing like smiles, we pipe and we swirl,
Creating bright critters that dance and twirl.
Laughter erupts as we craft and we mold,
Our treats are like treasures, a sight to behold!

Euphoria on a Plate and Laughter Untamed

Cookies are shaped like our wildest dreams,
With sprinkles that sparkle and sweet sugary beams!
Every bite's a giggle, a flavor explosion,
With each silly grin, we make our own potion.

Chocolate chips tumble like laughter on high,
Oh, who needs perfection? Just watch the gooey fly!
We bake up joy with each messy splash,
In this season of cheer, we create quite the clash!

The Heartfelt Bakes of the Year

Laughter fills bowls as we frolic with sweets,
Mixing up fun in our favorite treats.
Grandma's old secrets sneak into the mix,
With a pinch of delight and a dash of sweet tricks.

Our tummies are rumbling, they can hardly wait,
For the magic we make, oh, we celebrate!
With flour on faces, we share hearty laughs,
These momentary blunders are our finest crafts!

Enchanted Sprouts of Sweet Wonder

A sprinkle of mischief, a dash of delight,
In ovens, our giggles burst into light.
Cookie creations, a whimsical race,
Frosted hilarity, we all embrace!

As we munch on the fails, it's all part of the fun,
With each silly flop, our hearts weigh a ton.
So bring out the sweets with their wild little quirks,
In this jolly bake-off, we're all just big jerks!

Frosted Fairy Tales of the Heart

In a kitchen where giggles rise,
The dough does dance, oh what a surprise!
Sugar sprinkles on noses snuck,
We're baking dreams, with all our luck.

The oven sings a merry tune,
While we twirl like a cartoon.
Piping bags make silly faces,
As we race through floury places.

The frosting flows like a wild stream,
Creating castles for every dream.
We laugh until our bellies ache,
This tasty magic we will make!

So eat your treats and let them go,
For laughter is the best flavor, you know!
In every bite, a giggle hides,
Frosted joys that the heart abides.

Seasonal Sweets in Cozy Nooks

In cozy corners filled with cheer,
The sweets appear as the holidays near.
With every nibble, a burst of fun,
Our merry chaos has just begun!

The cats get tangled in ribbon threads,
As we decorate with sugar spreads.
Cookies look like they've gone awry,
With crooked smiles as they wave goodbye.

Hot cocoa spills with a frothy splash,
Marshmallows leap in a fluffy clash.
We giggle at the sights we create,
Baking mishaps that just can't wait!

So gather round your favorite chairs,
With treats and laughter, no one dares,
To take the holidays too serious,
When festive fun is quite delirious!

Echoes of Joy Through Whisk and Dough

In a whirl of dough, we spin and twirl,
With cookie cutters, our joy unfurl.
A sprinkle here, a pinch of glee,
Each laugh resounds like a sweet decree!

Mom's rolling pin creates a tune,
As flour flurries around the room.
With every whisk, our hearts take flight,
Creating memories, pure delight!

The icing drizzles like waterfall streams,
While we share our most silly dreams.
With sugary hearts and laughter loud,
We bake our wishes under the crowd.

So gather 'round and raise a cheer,
For joys of baking that bring us near.
In every cookie, a hug we send,
With laughter and love that will not end!

Batches of Bliss under Twinkling Stars

Under starlit skies, we gather tight,
Mixing up troubles with pure delight.
With laughter ringing as we stir,
Creating bliss that makes us purr.

The kitchen glows with a friendly spark,
While dough balls roll to their merry mark.
With giggles fluffy as the puffed treats,
We skip and hop to the rhythm of beats.

Marzipan shapes seem to come alive,
As we compete to see who can thrive.
"Mine's the best!" we playfully claim,
While tasting victories — it's all the same!

So let's toast to fun and silly flair,
With every bite, we share and dare.
Under twinkling stars, our joy remains,
Batches of bliss in festive frames.

Candy-Flecked Hopes and Hearthside Whispers

In a kitchen filled with giggles and mess,
A cookie disaster, oh what a stress.
Sprinkles fly as we dance and we bake,
Creating a treat that's bound to mistake.

Flour on noses, we're quite the sight,
Tasting the batter, oh pure delight.
We laugh till it hurts, it's all in fun,
Who cares if the cookies are overdone?

Candies melt into each other's dreams,
Sweetest of laughter in sugary schemes.
Hearthside whispers as the oven hums,
Waiting for treats, but here comes the crumbs!

So we sing carols off-key and loud,
Proud of our chaos, we laugh unbowed.
In this festive mess, joy's on display,
With fuzzy memories to warm the day.

Cinnamon Swirls and Cozy Nights

The cinnamon swirls are twirling away,
While we sip hot cocoa and happily sway.
With marshmallows floating like fluffy clouds,
And laughter erupting, we're a merry crowd.

The cat steals a bun, oh what a scene!
As we chase him around, it's a comical routine.
Under blankets we squish, all cozy and warm,
With giggles and tickles, it's laughter we're sworn.

The timer beeps loud, calling us back,
To cookies we baked, though we lost the track.
Each bite brings a smile, full of cheer,
Sharing a joke is my favorite part here.

As outside it snows, the chill's in the air,
Inside it's all warmth and good times to share.
In this season of joy, with a sprinkle of spice,
We'll cherish these moments that feel oh-so-nice.

Twinkling Lights and Sweet Delights

Twinkling lights dance on the window pane,
As we nibble on sweets while avoiding the rain.
With chocolate-dipped fingers, we create our art,
This sweet little chaos is close to my heart.

The puppy's been eyeing our frosting stash,
As we laugh and he steals a bite in a flash.
He's got chocolate on his snout, what a sight,
We can't help but giggle in this joyous night.

Candles alight, as stories unfold,
Each tale brings a chuckle, like treasures of gold.
With each cheerful bite, happiness grows,
In the warmth of the season, our laughter flows.

So here's to the moments both wild and sweet,
In the glow of the lights, we gather to eat.
With cookies and giggles that brighten the dark,
This holiday season ignites a sweet spark.

The Scent of Cheer Beneath the Snow

The scent of cheer wafts under the snow,
As we dream of treats in this frosty glow.
With sugar on fingers and laughter embraced,
In this winter wonderland, our fun is well-paced.

Mittens on feet, we slide on the floor,
Chasing the crumbs we can't help but adore.
While frosting melts in a sweet little fight,
Coziness sings through the chilly night.

Tinsel hangs wildly, the tree's looking bright,
While cookie mischief brings pure delight.
In moments like these, with love all around,
Our hearts are aglow in joy that we've found.

So let's raise a glass to sugar and spice,
In this holiday whirl, every moment's precise.
With giggles and warmth as we snuggle up tight,
May laughter and joy be our guiding light.

Meringue Magic and Candied Wishes

In the kitchen, chaos reigns,
Flour flies like falling rains,
Eggs are cracked with silly sounds,
Laughter echoes all around.

Spoons are sticky, hands a mess,
Churning dreams of sugary bliss.
Buttercream battles on the floor,
Who knew baking could be a chore?

Cookies shaped like silly hats,
Frosted smiles for silly chaps.
The oven hums a jolly tune,
As we dance beneath the moon.

Sprinkles flying overhead,
Wishing for a sugar spread.
With every bite, we burst with glee,
Oh, what a sweet jamboree!

Cozy Corners and Sweet Spells

In cozy corners, secrets stir,
Hot cocoa warms with a gentle purr.
With marshmallows dancing on the top,
We share our giggles, never stop.

Candles flicker, shadows prance,
A chocolate fountain makes us dance.
Caramel rivers flow with cheer,
We toast the season, spread the cheer.

Funny faces made of dough,
Who knew cookies could steal the show?
In every bite, a joke unfolds,
Laughter mixed with cinnamon gold.

Our table, a feast of silly dreams,
With frosting laughter that surely beams.
A sprinkle here, a laugh right there,
Cozy corners, we have our share!

Frosty Ends and Velvet Beginnings

Winter winds bring playful sights,
Snowflakes dancing, oh what delights!
A ginger snap with a peppered grin,
Frosty tales where fun begins.

Velvet ribbons wrapped so tight,
Holiday cheer takes its flight.
With every tickle and playful shove,
We bake our joy with frothy love.

Jolly tales of sweetness shared,
With cookie crumbs, nothing cared.
The snowmen chuckle from outside,
Inside, we giggle, full of pride.

Mittens soggy, noses red,
We'll munch on treats 'til we're all fed.
Who needs a feast when fun's the prize?
In our frosty, sugary pies!

Peppermint Swirls and Mirthful Twirls

In the air, a peppermint flair,
Giggling kids without a care.
Twirling dough like a dizzy breeze,
Sprinkling sugar with such ease.

Candy canes in silly fights,
Dancing cookies on festive nights.
Chasing sprinkles, they scatter wide,
With jolly hearts, we take a ride.

Tales of laughter, the sweetest sound,
Sugar plums in dreams abound.
Each bite a chuckle, each laugh a cheer,
Mirthful twirls, we hold so dear.

So grab a tray and join the fun,
With frosted snacks for everyone.
In this swirl of treat-filled bliss,
We find our joy, not one we miss!

A Smidgen of Spice

In the kitchen, chaos reigns,
Flour flies like little grains.
I've added cinnamon, quite a dash,
Watch the cookies rise in a flash.

The oven beeps, I have to run,
But wait! What's that? What's come undone?
A cat has launched into the mix,
Now my cookies are in a fix.

I sprinkle sugar, hoping for luck,
But somehow dough's stuck like muck.
My masterpiece, a wobbly sight,
Yet it will taste divine tonight.

A Splash of Cheer

Candies scatter all around,
On the counter, joy is found.
Chocolate chips and jelly beans,
The messiest of cooking scenes.

I pour the milk, it spills with glee,
'Tis a lovely tragedy, you see?
Sprinkling sprinkles, oh what fun,
It's like a party for everyone.

I taste a bit, and oh so sweet,
My ginger treat is quite a feat.
Though maybe next time, I'll not dive,
Into baking like I'm in a jive.

Warm Wishes in Every Bite.

Rolling dough in every nook,
Got the recipe from a book.
But it seems my math's a mess,
I've made a cake, I must confess.

Frosting squiggles on my face,
A playful take on a baking race.
I try to frost with style and grace,
But end up looking like a case.

With every bite, a laugh I get,
Surprises lurk in every set.
These treats bring joy, a giggle spree,
Even with icing on my knee.

Sugar Spice and Everything Nice

Laughter bubbles as we bake,
Trying hard, but what a shake!
Sugar clouds and frosty whisk,
I'm a baker? Oh, what a risk!

Mixing flavors, such delight,
More chocolate? Oh, that's just right!
Yet somehow I've made a soup,
Which is not quite the goal of the group.

We taste the mix, it's quite absurd,
But who needs rules? Let's spread the word.
With a giggle and a frosted smear,
We chime in joy, it's holiday cheer!

Frosted Dreams in Winter's Embrace

The snowflakes fall, a perfect scene,
But in my kitchen, it's quite the queen.
Buttercream battles on my shirt,
I'm covered in frosting, yes, it's hurt!

Mixing flavors, aiming for cheer,
But my spatula has disappeared!
Found it stuck to the ceiling, oh dear,
Guess that's proof that fun is near!

When cookies sing with sugar tunes,
We laugh together like silly loons.
Frosted dreams we'll bake tonight,
Who needs neat? We'll take this flight!

Holiday Joys Wrapped in Lavender

Baking goods with lulled intent,
My cat's in flour, a mess well-spent.
Chasing crumbs, my dog's in glee,
While I pronounce, 'This is fancy!'

Sprinkling sugar, not too high,
The dough's rebellious, oh my, oh my!
Dripping icing, what a sight,
I swear this cookie's taking flight!

Milk and cocoa fill the scene,
As we dance, a sugar dream.
Mom's got recipes worth a look,
But ends up with a quirky cook!

Laughter bounces off each wall,
As we serve that odd-looking ball.
With jokes and puns, the fun won't stop,
We toast to failures - cheers! Now pop!

Mystical Flavors of Cinnamon Nights

In the oven, something brews,
The smell of chaos, and our shoes.
Baker's cap and apron on tight,
We mix and stir until midnight.

Cinnamon sticks, a playful tease,
My brother's dancing with great ease.
Flour fights ignite the air,
I wonder how he got that hair!

Rolling dough like a wild spree,
A cookie monster waits for me.
I sprinkle sprinkles like confetti,
Praying the results aren't too sweaty!

Nighttime giggles fill our hearts,
As culinary magic departs.
We take a bite, it's quite a mix,
We feast on all our kitchen tricks!

Twinkling Delights and Cheery Smiles

Creating wonders, oh what fun,
My sister giggles while we run.
The dough, it fights against my hand,
This cookie's shy, won't take a stand.

Frosting bright as Rudolph's nose,
Splatters on toes, not just on clothes.
We laugh and dab at the frosty goo,
And decorate the pup, who says 'moo'?

With jolly faces, each bite's a joy,
Our cookies risky, like a toy.
We munch and crunch with wild delight,
What a bizarre, scrumptious sight!

Sharing moments, laughter loud,
Standing tall, we're cookie proud.
And what a joy, this messy scene,
A holiday party fit for a queen!

Sweet Hearths and Warm Fires

Gather round, it's story time,
With gooey treats and joy sublime.
The marshmallows dance in the pot,
While Dad attempts his s'mores, what a shot!

We sip hot cocoa, so divine,
My brother spills some on the line.
Laughter erupts as we sip and slosh,
Mom shines brightly like a posh squash!

Candles flicker, stories blur,
Each tale a mishap, each laugh a spur.
We toss the crusts and share the crust,
In this warm love, there's never mistrust.

So here we are, a lofty crew,
Baking dreams, both false and true.
With smiles and hopes, we light the night,
In cozy kitchens, our hearts take flight!

The Mirth of Spiced Cheery Treats

In a kitchen bustling, oh what a sight,
The cookies are dancing, all through the night.
Frosting is flying, the sprinkles take flight,
Giggling and munching, it feels just right.

Laughter erupts as the dough starts to squish,
Who knew that making could bring such a wish?
With each little bite, a sugary swish,
Whisking away all the woes we dismiss.

Merry faces smeared with sweet delight,
Chomping on goodies, with pure appetite.
The more we bake, the more we invite,
Joy in our hearts, and that's just polite.

With a pinch of this and a dash of that,
We laugh as we wear our floury hats.
Snack time's a frenzy, all paws, and a pat,
In the mirth of treats, we can't help but chat.

Warm Embraces in Frosty Air

Under blankets thick, we snuggle so tight,
Outside is all frosty, but oh what a sight.
Hot cocoa in cups, marshmallows in flight,
Tickles and giggles, our hearts feel so light.

Snowflakes are dancing, they twirl and they spin,
We're bundled up cozy, let the fun begin.
With each little sip, we have a big grin,
Frosty air does wonders, oh where to begin?

Bursting with laughter, we roll in the snow,
Our cheeks rosy red, and cheeks aglow.
Sledding down hills, oh what a show,
In warm embraces, our spirits will grow.

As twinkling lights flicker, we cheer and we cheer,
A season of laughter that draws us all near.
Through chilly nights, our friendships are dear,
In warm frosty breezes, we cast off all fear.

Sugarplum Serenades and Laughter

In a world of sweet dreams on sugarplum toes,
Dancing around as the sweet holiday glows.
Melodies ring out, as the fun ebbs and flows,
Laughter ignites, where delight ever grows.

With each tiny bite, a symphony rings,
Cupcakes and cookies like joyful little kings.
Dressed up in sprinkles, our happiness swings,
In concerts of flavor, nostalgia it brings.

Chortles and chuckles in every thin slice,
Biting down joy; oh, how nice is the spice!
Songs of the season, how tasty and trice,
Singing with glee; oh, take my advice!

As the yard fills with laughter, from dusk until dawn,
With sugar-coasted friends, the worries are gone.
In a whirlwind of joy, as we gladly fawn,
Sweet serenades linger, till the last light is drawn.

Cookies and Cocoa Under Stardust

Cookies in jars, lined up on the shelf,
Cocoa in mugs, oh let's treat ourselves!
With stardust above, we giggle and delve,
Into the delights that we crafted ourselves.

Marshmallows float like clouds in the sky,
We take silly sips, and the time flutters by.
Sugar dusted cheeks as we laugh and we sigh,
Underneath twinkling stars, our spirits fly high.

The smell of the sweets dances through the night,
With each little nibble, everything feels right.
Sprinkling some joy as we share our delight,
In a world full of wonders, our hearts are so light.

Gather round, friends, for a holiday cheer,
With cookies and cocoa, we'll toast without fear.
In laughter and joy, everything is clear,
Under the stardust, we sing loud and near.

Magical Confections and Yuletide Reflections

In the kitchen, chaos reigns,
Flour clouds and sticky stains.
A cookie monster takes his stand,
With rolling pins held in each hand.

Laughter bounces off the walls,
As sprinkles tumble, candy falls.
Frosting castles for each knight,
In frosting armor, such a sight!

The oven dings, the treats arise,
Some look cute, some win the prize.
A flavor fight breaks out in glee,
As taste buds dance like leaves from trees.

We toast to sweets, a funny cheer,
With every bite, we banish fear.
For in this joyful, silly mess,
We find the magic of each bless.

Sweetness in the Air and Laughter Everywhere

Sugar plums on little toes,
Frosty noses greet us close.
Cookies giggle, chocolates moan,
In every corner, sweetness grown.

Muffins jump and pancakes waltz,
Syrup rivers, none can halt.
We rollick round in merry song,
Oh, how the treats all get along!

A pie that's singing 'slice me now',
A ginger snap, a curious cow.
Smiles and giggles fill the space,
As we embrace this sweet embrace.

With whisks a-whirling, laughs erupt,
Cream-cheese frosting in a cup.
For every bite brings jokes anew,
In candy land, we shake and stew.

Whipped Cream Wishes on Starry Nights

Underneath the twinkling lights,
Whipped cream clouds take silly flights.
Marshmallow fluff in fluffy hats,
As cocoa sips and giggles chat.

S'more stacks are towering high,
Chocolate rivers near by.
With every bite, a grin would form,
Sweet surprises are the norm.

Don't forget the cherry red,
That wobbles on a cookie bed.
The laughter echoes, spun like gold,
As spicy tales of goodies told.

All the wishes dance and swirl,
Tales of sugar in a twirl.
With every sip, with every cheer,
Starry nights bring us so near.

Cheery Spice and Winter's Glow

Pumpkin pies and cookies tin,
Spicy laughter, let's begin.
Cinnamon sticks in every cup,
Smiling friends who lift us up.

Marzipan with funny faces,
In our hearts, we find warm places.
Nutmeg sprinkles bring a grin,
As laughter bubbles from within.

Warm and cozy, hugs abound,
In every corner, joy is found.
With flour in our wild hair,
We bake with love, sans any care.

In this whimsical, sugar dance,
We twirl and kick, we sing, we prance.
For in this season, oh so bright,
Spice it up with pure delight!

Sweet Serenity on Winter's Breath

In a kitchen warm with cheer,
Cookies dance, oh what a year!
Flour flies and giggles rise,
Baking dreams in sweet disguise.

Marshmallow snowmen grin so wide,
While frosting rivers take a ride.
Laughter echoes, joy's parade,
Sugar sprinkles, plans are made.

The oven hums a festive tune,
As we pretend it's always June.
Spices twirl like dancers bright,
In a whirlwind of pure delight.

With every bite, we joke and tease,
Crumbs and giggles, oh yes, please!
Sweetness fills the frosty air,
In this season, we have flair.

Frost-kissed Treats on the December Wind

Snowflakes tumble, spices blend,
With every laugh, our worries mend.
Pies in the oven, oh what a sight,
Doughnuts with sprinkles make it right.

Chasing each other, who can resist?
Licking the bowl is quite a twist.
The cat steals a treat, we all shout,
'Get that furry thief out!'

Candies piled up like a dream,
Can't resist that sugar beam.
Chocolate rivers flowing wide,
Baking blunders can't hide our pride.

So grab a plate, let's share a laugh,
Pastry chaos, a sweetened path.
In every cookie, a heart beats fast,
Together we'll ensure this joy will last.

Hearts and Hearths Wrapped in Delight

By the glow of fire, we all sing,
Ginger snaps that make hearts cling.
Sipping cocoa, marshmallows in tow,
With each sip, our laughter will grow.

Who needs socks when cookies are here?
Dancing with flour takes away fear.
Each cookie break has a funny twist,
Who knew baking could cause such bliss?

Trees are lit with cheerful glow,
As we sneak bites, shh! Don't let it show.
Laughter fills the cozy room,
Where every mishap spells out our zoom.

So let's create our merry mess,
In this season, we are blessed.
Wrapped in warmth, we take our place,
Creating memories we will embrace.

Sprinkling Joy in Every Thought

Sugar crunch and a little cheer,
What's that smell? The best time of year!
Cookies stacked like little hills,
Each one grinning, giving thrills.

With icing guns, we draw and play,
Decorating treats in a silly way.
'That one's a monster!' one claims in jest,
While icing battles put skills to test.

Sprinkles fly like winter snow,
Who knew cookies could steal the show?
In every laugh and silly dance,
We find ourselves in a joyful trance.

So gather close, let's share a bite,
With every cookie, hearts take flight.
In this sweet chaos, our joy's unfurled,
As we spread laughter across the world.

Dusted with Sugar and Sprinkled with Love

In a kitchen where giggles stir,
A flour fight we can't deter.
Rolling pins launch with a clack,
Dough's flying forward, no turning back!

Cookie cutters dance with flair,
Frosted faces everywhere.
Sprinkles rain from all around,
Laughter's the sweetest sound!

Burnt edges laugh with pride,
But sweet joy we cannot hide.
Each nibble brings a giggly cheer,
'Tis the season; we have no fear!

Sugar plums looking oddly round,
In this bakery, fun's abound.
With each bite, our troubles flee,
Here's to joy and sticky glee!

Flourishing Hopes in the Frosty Beyond

Baking dreams on a cold, bright day,
While mischief wraps us in its sway.
With each whisk, a silly jest,
Frosting fights? Oh, we're the best!

Snowflakes swirl, oh what a sight,
But we're stuck inside, feeling light.
A cupcake war in the pantry's space,
Found icing smeared on a puppy's face!

Cinnamon giggles bubble and bloom,
As we dance around the living room.
Each sweet treat tells tales of fun,
Chasing shadows, we all run!

With cookie crumbles on our cheeks,
Happiness plays hide-and-seek.
In this festive baking spree,
We find our joy like bees to tea!

Candied Memories in the Making

Whisking memories into a bowl,
With candy sprinkles on a roll.
Laughter mixes with the dough,
Making frosty visions flow!

Nose deep in an oven's glow,
Oh, the sugary tales we know.
Chocolate chips like tiny stars,
Mark our journey, oh how far!

Fluffy marshmallows float in the air,
Creating laughter without a care.
Muffins rise like our dreams,
With giggles bursting at the seams!

Let's stash away the serious face,
Here we bake in pure embrace.
Candied moments, a sweet parade,
In this festive, joyous charade!

Hearth Hearths and Sweet Serenades

In a cozy corner where cookies bake,
We sing tunes that make hearts quake.
Marshmallow lyrics fill the air,
With frosting sprinkled everywhere!

Ginger snaps tap dance on the floor,
As laughter swirls through every door.
With a dash of whimsy and a pinch of fun,
We bake until all day is done!

Stirring joy with a wooden spoon,
Our friendship fills the room like a tune.
With each bite, a chorus rings,
It's the silly joy that baking brings!

So raise a mug of cocoa high,
Let our giggles reach the sky.
In this oven of love we thrive,
Baking together keeps us alive!

Festive Bakes & Gleeful Mirth

In the kitchen, flour flies,
Whisking eggs 'neath joyful sighs.
The cake, it jiggles, what a sight,
A merry dance, we bake in fright.

Oh, the pies with crusts like gold,
Sugar rushes never get old.
We laugh at crumbs on every chair,
Sprinkled smiles are everywhere!

Muffins puffing, rising high,
Like our hopes, they touch the sky.
Bakers with dough upon their nose,
Who knew our art would have such prose?

When we feast, it's pure delight,
With every bite, we reach new heights.
A cheer for sweets and silly fun,
In this kitchen, joy's begun!

Whipped Cream Dreams and Starry Skies

Marshmallows dancing in the air,
Syrupy laughter everywhere.
A spoon takes flight, oh what a mess,
Sweet chaos, I must confess!

Sprinkles scattered like confetti,
Wobbling jellies, aren't they pretty?
Whipped cream mountains piled up high,
Dessert dreams that make us sigh!

Candies jostling for a place,
In this wild and wondrous race.
Sugar rushes, giggles blend,
Every bite, our woes suspend.

Under stars, our wishes soar,
To the moon and then some more.
With sticky fingers, we make a pact,
For each sweet dream, that's a fact!

Hearthside Tales of Sweet Reverie

By the fire, giggles roam,
Cookies crumbling, we feel at home.
With tales of yore that twist and twine,
Every crackle is a sign.

Marzipan figures start to sing,
Baked delights that make hearts spring.
Chocolate rivers flow with ease,
Imaginations dance in the breeze.

Nutty bites and frosty treats,
Hearthside laughter, oh, what feats!
With every munch, a tale's begun,
In our feast, we are all one.

As marshmallow clouds drift by,
We tell our stories, oh so spry.
Spiced wishes warming our souls,
In this cozy nook, we find our goals!

Cookies Crumbling Like Time

Once we baked a towering cake,
But frosting spilled—oh, for goodness' sake!
We laughed until we nearly cried,
Sweet disasters, we won't hide!

Cookies crumbled like our plans,
Sugar spritzers in our hands.
With every bite and every laugh,
We create our own photograph!

Chocolate chunks and stories shared,
In this kitchen, we are spared.
Burnt edges are badges of pride,
In every crumb, our dreams reside.

As we bake and cheer and play,
Time ticks by, we shoo it away.
With gooey hands and hearts so bright,
In this moment, we take flight!

Mirthful Moments by the Fireside

On a chair made of candy, I'm stuck like glue,
With a mug full of chocolate, I sip and chew.
My socks are mismatched; they dance on the floor,
While marshmallows frolic; oh, what a roar!

The cat in a sweater, a sight so absurd,
From the tree, tinsel hangs like a big, shiny bird.
Uncles tell tales that may not be true,
While Auntie attempts a strange jingle or two.

Popcorn ribbons swinging, sweet chaos unfolds,
A lopsided snowman, with a heart made of gold.
Who knew that the fun could grow more each year?
With giggles and wishes, we spread so much cheer!

So here's to the nights filled with warmth and delight,
With family and friends snugly tucked in tight.
The laughter and joy, oh, how they ignite,
In a kaleidoscope dance of the season so bright!

Ecstasy of Edible Ornaments

A cookie-shaped ornament hangs oh so low,
Tempting my fingers to nibble and go.
Grandma's creations all lined up in rows,
Each one a treasure that squeals with 'Who knows?'

Frosting explosions, like art gone awry,
With sprinkles like confetti that soar to the sky.
The dog swipes a cupcake, oh what a scene!
As we laugh, there's crumbs scattered like dreams.

A countdown of treats makes my tummy do flips,
Every bite a journey; I take little trips.
Ginger snaps in knickknacks, what a delight,
With gumdrops all giggling in the soft, mellow light.

Let's bake and create with glee and a grin,
With recipes tangled like yarn made of sin.
We'll munch on our spoils, oh what a fine plan,
In the glorious chaos of our sweet little clan!

Spice-laden Fantasies on Frost-tipped Evenings

Sprinkling cinnamon in an even mix,
We conjure up laughter with some playful tricks.
The ginger snap brigade forms an army of cheer,
Marching through sugar, claiming the year!

Pine cones take hats, and we giggle with glee,
As the chocolaty treats unleash jubilee.
A snowman demands a taste, snowballs and cream,
His carrot nose giggling; it's all just a dream!

As bells jingle madly, la-la-la, what a sound!
We dance like the cookies that spin round and round.
With giggles and sparklers, the night is alive,
As the tasty delights hungry dreams contrive.

The cocoa flows strong, with swirls and some zest,
Add a dash of pure joy; it's a sugary fest!
So let's raise a toast, with marshmallows bright,
To evenings so whimsical, glowing with light!

Delights in the Chill of December

In cozy corners, we gather and chat,
While snowflakes compose tunes in a dance like a cat.
With mittens of reindeer and hats full of cheer,
Who knew the cold could taste so sincere?

As peppermint dreams swirl in the air,
The scent of pine needles lingers everywhere.
Vents puffing giggles, what a merry song,
As popcorn chains hang, right where they belong.

A splat of hot cider on my favorite shirt,
I laugh as it dribbles; oh, this little flirt!
The elves in the kitchen add spice to our fun,
With laughter a recipe that brightens the sun.

So let's share the joy, spread laughter like jam,
With each quirky moment, we laugh and we slam.
December so funny, with all its embrace,
Bringing friends together, a warm, wondrous space!

Enchanted Frostings and Twinkling Lights

Under the glow, a cookie parade,
Frosted faces, a sweet charade.
Sprinkles like stars, they dance in delight,
In this tasty frenzy, all night is bright.

Laughter erupts as the dough starts to jig,
The pillows of sugar, we dance a big gig.
With ginger snaps twirling and icing so bright,
The kitchen's our stage, what a marvelous sight!

Oh, the sugar high is a lovely delight,
Gummy bears sing, what a silly plight.
As the cat claims a cookie, a heist in full force,
We're giggling around as we plot our sweet course.

So raise up a spatula, let's all take a bite,
With toppings aplenty, we'll snicker and bite.
These twinkling creations, a hilarious cheer,
With frosting so sticky, let's spread out the cheer!

Whimsical Tastes of Yule

Sprinkles and giggles adorn every treat,
With marshmallows dancing, they sway on their feet.
My mom made a reindeer, it's missing an ear,
But who needs perfection when laughter is near?

The chocolate river flows, oh what a sight,
With elves on ice skates, sliding with fright.
My cookie had legs, and it took off to run,
Chasing the dog, oh what goofy fun!

Bubbles of laughter fill up every room,
While cupcakes are plotting a sugary boom.
If frosting could giggle, it surely would burst,
As we munch on whatever our sweet tooth has cursed!

So let's raise a glass filled with fizzy delight,
To cakes that do flips, oh what a sweet flight!
In delightfully madness, we should take a pause,
For nothing's as funny as dessert by the paws!

Frosty Lane of Memories and Merriment

Down the frosty lane, we skip and we trudge,
With glee on our faces, our hearts we won't judge.
A snowman of cookies, his nose made of cheese,
He wobbles and giggles, melting the freeze.

Tiny hands sprinkle, with chocolate galore,
As we deck the halls with a sticky rapport.
Laughter echoes as we mix up the dough,
Going in circles, the flour does blow!

The cat's in the basket, wrapped tight with some fluff,
Looking like Santa, just a bit too chuff.
While tinsel hangs low and the lights flicker bright,
Even the ornaments grin at our plight!

So gather 'round friends, let's whip up some cheer,
With giggles and goodies, the reason is clear.
As we make merry mischief, this time of the year,
It's funnier still with a slice of cold beer!

Baked Love and Twinkling Joys

In our cozy kitchen, a battering scene,
With love in our hearts, we make quite the cuisine.
Cookies in chaos, oh what a delight,
With flour on noses, we're ready to bite!

No rules 'round here, just a sprinkle of cheer,
With giggly mishaps, and yelps loud and clear.
My cake sprung a leak, like a soda gone wild,
But laughter erupts like the joy of a child!

A cupcake's a hat, so absurdly arranged,
Worn by the dog, who looks so deranged.
The oven's a dragon, it roars and it puffs,
As we dance in the heat, oh, enough is enough!

So grab your spatula, let's stir up some fun,
The joy of our baking, second to none.
With every sweet bite, and each twinkling sight,
We'll feast till we laugh, in the warmth of the night!

Flavors of the Season and Joy on Repeat

In the kitchen, the chaos reigns,
Cookies piling high like candy canes,
Flour on faces, laughter fills the air,
Baking blunders, who will prepare?

Sprinkles flying like confetti bright,
Frosting battles in the soft moonlight,
Taste testers with frosting on their nose,
A sweet disaster everyone knows!

Mixing up flavors, a dash of surprise,
Who knew that cereal could be so wise?
Chocolate chips rolling where they don't belong,
A funny frenzy, our goofy song!

With giggles and grumbles, the oven's a friend,
As doughnuts masquerade, the fun won't end,
Joy on repeat, we'll savor this feast,
With silly smiles, our laughter increased!

The Magic of Meringue at Midnight

Underneath the stars, we whisk with glee,
Egg whites peak high, just wait and see,
The clock strikes twelve, is that a rubber chicken?
Meringue on the ceiling, oh it's quite the trickin'!

Frosty delights catching a moonlit glow,
Baking with friends is the way to go,
Sticky fingers, we're giggling aloud,
Whipped cream disasters, oh we're so proud!

Spoons clanging, what an amusing affair,
Sugar and spice fly through the air,
With each swirl and twirl, a laugh we ignite,
Midnight magic, oh, what a sight!

Like fairies we dance in a sugar rush,
In the hilarity, we all proudly hush,
But with each bite, our troubles we toss,
For meringue in madness, we are the boss!

Sugarplum Dreams and Frosty Fantasies

In the land of sweets, where dreams ignite,
Sugarplum fairies take flight at night,
Frosty desserts glide in a comical spin,
With a sprinkle of laughter, let the games begin!

Marshmallow snowmen standing so tall,
Melting away with a giggle and fall,
Whipped cream fights on the frostbitten floor,
As we raid the pantry for just one more!

Cookies in costumes, what a sight to behold,
Doughnut snowballs, our treasures of gold,
With every sweet bite, a tangle we weave,
Creating a feast that no one can leave!

And as the clock chimes, we twirl with delight,
In this frosty realm, everything's light,
Sugarplum dreams and fantasies tease,
With hearty laughter, we're sure to please!

Celebratory Cravings in the Glittering Night

In a glimmering hurry, the kitchen's alive,
Mixing up memories, we all dive,
A whirl of chocolate, sprinkles, and cheer,
Counting our blessings as friends gather near!

Gathered around the table, what a view,
Cakes with balloons, and icing with glue,
Sugar-coated giggles bounce here and there,
Life's a banquet, let's share our flair!

Sipping hot cocoa, as marshmallows float,
Ideas and laughter, sweet treats we gloat,
Celebratory cravings, we're in a trance,
With every bite taken, we jump and we dance!

As the stars twinkle over our sugary fun,
We bake through the night until the rise of the sun,
Full of sweet stories and joy in our plight,
In the glittering night, everything's bright!

Sugar-Spiced Dreams

In a world of flour and sweet delight,
Where cookies dance in the pale moonlight,
Sugar sprinkles rain down from the sky,
As ginger folk giggle and wink their eye.

They frolic and play, so jolly and spry,
Dancing on rooftops, oh me, oh my!
With icing smiles and peppermint cheer,
Every bite brings laughter, oh dear, oh dear!

Sipping hot cocoa, we toast with glee,
To the sugary magic that sets us free.
A sprinkle of joy with each yummy treat,
Who knew that dessert could be so sweet?

Their sugary dreams, they keep us awake,
While making us giggle with every quake.
So grab a warm cookie, give it a toss,
In the land of delights where we are the boss!

Frosted Hugs Beneath the Mistletoe

Underneath the green and fluffy pine,
A frosty surprise that tastes divine.
Kisses made of chocolate, oh what a sight,
Who knew the holidays could be such a bite?

Muffin men marching with gingerbread swords,
While jolly old elves sing sweet little chords.
Laughter erupts, it echoes all around,
As snowy confections blanket the ground.

With marshmallow clouds and licorice streams,
We hustle and bustle, chasing our dreams.
For every silly slip on the cold, slick floor,
We giggle and grumble, but always want more!

The hugs we share, laced with icing and cheer,
Beneath the mistletoe, we lose all fear.
With each silly moment, we cuddle up tight,
In this whimsical world, everything's right!

Sweet Echoes of Winter Whispers

The winter air is crisp and bright,
With sugarplum fairies taking flight.
They giggle and swoosh through frosty trees,
While candy canes sway with the gentle breeze.

Whispers of laughter swirl through the night,
As ginger folks tumble, oh what a sight!
Each frosted cookie hides a sly little grin,
Let's hope we don't crumble before we begin!

Hot chocolate rivers flow through the towns,
While everyone wears their sweet tooth crowns.
Frosty nose and rosy cheeks,
We summon the joy that winter seeks.

As we dance around, giggling galore,
We gather our treasures and bounce off the floor.
These echoes of sweetness echo our dreams,
In this jolly season, nothing's as it seems!

Cozy Nights and Candy Delights

In cozy corners, we settle in tight,
With candy galore, a delightful sight!
Gummy bears bouncing on pillows of fluff,
As we dig into sweets, never enough!

Marshmallows puffing like clouds up high,
We throw them in cocoa, watch them comply.
Each melting moment fills us with cheer,
On these delightful nights, we conquer our fears.

Amidst the giggles and sugary haze,
We play silly games, creating our ways.
With laughter and snacks, the hours fly by,
As we nibble on dreams that tickle the sky.

So here's to the nights wrapped in sweet bliss,
Where every warm hug feels like a kiss.
In our cozy cocoon, we share gleeful sights,
Celebrating the magic of candy-filled nights!

Moonlit Mixes and Holiday Mirth

Under the moon, we dance and sway,
With floury hands in a cheeky play.
Laughter rises, oh, what a sight,
Cookies flung in the soft twilight.

The dough spills over, what a mess!
Joyful chaos—who needs finesse?
Sprinkles rain down like glittering stars,
Sugar high, we'll race our jars!

Frosting fights and frosting fights,
Sweet smiles spread like sugary lights.
With giggles that pop like baked dough,
Our holiday spirit begins to glow!

So here's to the fun, let laughter thrive,
In moonlit mixes, we feel alive.
With a bite of our treats, we won't regret,
This merry mayhem, our best duet!

Cookies Under the Starry Sky

Under the stars, we bake by night,
With cookie dough that gives us delight.
A pinch of chaos, a sprinkle of cheer,
With each tasty nibble, we shout, "Oh dear!"

Caramel drips and chocolate flakes,
Laughter erupts from delicious mistakes.
Rolling and tumbling with dough on our face,
It's a cookie caper, a joyful race!

The moon winks down with its silvery glow,
As we snack on the treats, our giggles flow.
With silly hats and aprons askew,
Each cookie a treasure in our quirky zoo!

So here's to fun beneath the vast sky,
With cookies galore that make us fly.
We'll feast and frolic in this sweet bliss,
With every bite, a magical kiss!

Snow-dusted Mirth and Sweet Nostalgia

In a snow-dusted world, we jump and spin,
With flour on faces, let the fun begin!
We roll out the dough, oh, what a delight,
Each cookie a treasure, each bite a delight!

Festive chaos in our cozy space,
Gooey goodness, we try not to race.
With a laugh that echoes like snowflakes' fall,
We cheer for the cookies, we'll taste them all!

When frosty winds whisper tales so sweet,
We remember each crumb and our dancing feet.
With silly faces and sprinkles aplenty,
We laugh through the night, feeling quite giddy!

So here's to the giggles we share and spread,
In a wonderland kitchen, far from our bed.
The joy of our baking, a fun-filled spree,
With memories made, and cookies, whee!

The Whispers of Warm Cravings

When the oven hums, it's a lively tune,
With butter and sugar, we'll make it boom!
Flour flies high, with giggles galore,
A dance in the kitchen, we can't ignore!

The scent of vanilla is wafting through,
As we cover each cookie with chocolatey goo.
We nibble and munch, with crumbs on our chin,
A sweet and silly game we all love to win!

When cravings arise, we add more and more,
With a sly little grin, we're baking up lore.
Sprinkles like stars on our sugary treats,
A whimsical feast that nobody beats!

So let the laughter and baking collide,
In this warm kitchen, let joy be our guide.
With every concoction, our hearts take flight,
In sweet cravings' embrace, we find pure delight!